FOREST BOOKS

CHEERLEADER FOR A FUNERAL

NINA CASSIAN (Renée Annie Ştefănescu) was born in 1924 in Galaţi, Romania. Her distinguished literary career began in 1947, with publication of her first poetry collection, *La Scara 1/1* (On the Scale of 1 to 1). Since then, she has published over fifty books, including works of fiction and children's books. Her poetry has been translated into many languages, and has been published in English in the collections *Lady of Miracles* (Cloud Marauder, 1985), *Call Yourself Alive?: Love Poems* (Forest, 1988) and *Life Sentence* (Anvil, 1990).

She is also a composer of chamber and symphonic music, and has worked as a journalist and film critic. She has translated into Romanian work by Shakespeare, Molière, Brecht, Celan, Apollinaire and Mayakovsky.

In 1985 she was invited to teach creative writing as a Visiting Professor at New York University. Whilst in America, her friend Gheorghe Ursu was arrested in Romania, and Cassian's satirical verses on the Ceauşescu regime were discovered in his diary. Ursu was tortured to death, and Cassian had no choice but to seek asylum in New York where she has lived ever since.

BRENDA WALKER'S career has been divided between the arts and education, her university studies being at London and Keele. During the last few years she has devoted herself to poetry in translation and has co-translated with Andrea Deletant a number of Romanian writers.

Cheerleader for a Funeral

POEMS

by

Nina Cassian

FOREST
BOOKS
London & Boston

Translated by Brenda Walker
with the author

PUBLISHED BY
FOREST BOOKS

20 Forest View, Chingford, London E4 7AY, UK
PO Box 312, Lincoln Centre, MA 01773, USA

FIRST PUBLISHED 1992

Typeset in Great Britain by Cover to Cover, Cambridge
Printed in Great Britain by BPCC Wheatons Ltd, Exeter

Translations © Forest Books, apart from those indicated
as translated by James Waller and Lidia Vianu
Original work © Nina Cassian
Cover illustration © Angela Martin

British Library Cataloguing in Publication Data:
A catalogue record for this book is
available from the British Library

ISBN 1 85610 013 8

Library of Congress Catalogue Card No:
92–72468

Forest Books gratefully acknowledges financial support for this
volume from the Arts Council of Great Britain

Nina Cassian

Contents

A Note on the Translations

I first met Nina Cassian at the Writers' Union in Bucharest during 1985, when Andrea Deletant and I were gathering material for an anthology of Romanian Women poets, *Silent Voices*. Since then I have had the good fortune to have her as a friend and mentor. Over the years we have discovered the pleasure of working together creatively, our first project being the collection of love poems *Call Yourself Alive?* (Forest 1988).

Cheerleader for a Funeral has been another exhilarating collaborative experience. With a linguistic versatility that makes a translator virtually redundant, Nina changes images or lines from her originals in order to make the English versions more fluent and expressive, sometimes almost creating a new poem as she does so. Yet in each instance the poem has become stronger and more relevant to the English ear. The long hours spent creating, correcting and editing through the night with Nina always leave me charged up rather than tired, for her originality and enthusiasm for the task generate even more creative energy.

As we worked together in New York on the final versions of these poems, we suddenly realised that it was the anniversary of the visit to New York, seven years before, which ended with unexpected exile from her country following the terrible events in pre-revolutionary Romania. In some way, then, *Cheerleader for a Funeral* seems to symbolise the triumphant defiance of this extraordinary woman, against all the odds.

Brenda Walker,
London, September 1992

ix

The poems in *Cheerleader for a Funeral*, some of which are as recent as August '92, are collected here for the first time in English translation.

'The Frog and Me', 'The Fourth Monkey' and 'Stuck' are translated by the author with James Waller.

'If I take two steps', 'Dedication' and 'Thrillers' are translated by the author with Lidia Vianu.

'Ars Poetica – a polemic', 'Language', and 'Three Dialogues' are written directly in English.

At Dawn

Dialectics

In my childhood
the girls would take my hand
spinning me round
till I stopped dead
in the most beautiful position possible.
I'd pose as if picking a flower
or like a bird, four sheets to the wind –
though actually I never could keep completely still:
due to my hesitant leg,
my fretting eyelashes,
I lost every time.

Today it's the same
I just can't freeze with a single move.
Even now, if they were to shoot me down
and kill me
I'd still keep moving
through the blue stripes of my dress
which would run and meander through the grass
like forty restless streams.

Dance

Dressed in blue, I could
turn in the wind,
insert myself gently
into immediate matter.

Dressed in green, I could
provoke a disaster
that would never have happened
dressed in alabaster.

Dressed in red, I could
trace a diagonal
from one shore to the other – well done! –
to help pass a diaphanous army.

Dressed in yellow, I could slide
to death's side
– and so on.

Passage to light

Frozen splendour!
Death falls majestically
on small weeds and leaves.
This is our way:
we taste the last sacrament
with bleeding mouths, with blossoming wounds.
So be it.
If it's a punishment – so be it.
If it's a challenge – so be it.
If this is the way to get to the light
through bitter frost,
then let our flesh and soul freeze.

Backwards

The past tense enters my meal,
chews in my place,
each mouthful is swallowed in advance.
'Has been' devours 'to be',
sequesters Cordelia's salt,
the word turns etymologically back.

I'd be happy to get rid
of my precious dowry,
my recollections,
to shake off my shoulders
that sumptuous mantle
embroidered with forests and deer,
with marine storms and clusters of grapes,
coated with golden fur
– too heavy that part of life I traversed,
I carry it as if a corpse
draped in Aprils, Julys, Octobers, Februaries . . .

Wood

In a piece of wood, there are
horses' heads, long drips of colour,
pale eyes painted
by the One Solemn Painter.

And bones: kneecaps, claviculae,
femurs, perfect rhymes,
mimics of certain ghosts
known as forests, (sometimes).

If I feel wood, beneath I sense
protests hurled
by all abrupt reliefs
against the bi-dimensional world.

In a piece of wood, there's
a thirsty time I can't quench,
perfect calculated fibre-cells.
If I touch wood with my lips,
I begin to grow like a branch.

Description of the hand

The fifth finger is an ornament.
The third one is symmetry's axle.
The thumb is meant to grab.
The fourth plays a lesser role.
The second is Adam's (and God's) forefinger.

New style

When Sunday becomes a usual, anonymous day,
(no matter how tired God was)
you feel like going off the handle,
grabbing an axe,
breaking heaven's gates, banks' vaults,
phone booths, marriages,
you want it to be a working day
by writing poems, vomitting crimes,
being chased by guardians and hounds,
making history bark at you –
and then, you wish to become
the God of the calendar,
the one who decides:
'It is Sunday,
people and sheep,
caterpillars and tides! . . .'

The south wind

The south wind was gradually cooling
the sea, nor did it spare us
but tried to crush our tent and love's seeds.
The south wind, that spreads
an immobile cold, shutting down sea's colours
yet not provoking it.
Wind from the south, with its frosted mouth.

We opposed it best we could:
by swimming vigorously, breaking the cold
with kisses, with the blood of our lips.
We raised orange tents
which burned like flames in the sunset
and we were shouting out with love
and were the wind's loudest foes . . .

But summer had only two colours:
yellow – not the corn, but sand.
Green – not the grass, but sea.
Between two sterilities
our love remained unshielded,
the storm dismantled our tent,
our blood grew silent.

Since then, every time I hear fishermen say:
'South wind's coming up!'
– I feel like an old warrior
indebted to his wounds.

Together

Oh, I'd utter ecstatic cries
if I was watching with you, through you,
these ragged waters, these stone chimerae;
my childhood would erupt through my skin
like scarlet fever,
my thighs be smeared with blood
as on the wedding night.
Oh, I'd utter heretic cries
before these deities banned from heaven
on our earth of mortals,
if I were with you, saint lover,
caught together in this slice of sea
like a rock,
like an eternal
kernel.

* * * With just two steps

With just two steps, I arouse a turmoil of insects.
They lie buried deep in grass's entrails,
suckling summer's juices, moving short segments,
the sauve insects and the devastating ones;
One step and the ground gushes with insects,
another, and I am clothed in insects
from sole to thigh to waist,
I wall myself up in their steady, hard, work,
in their insisting flight, they transform me
into a statue of insects, a humming column
in memory of summer.

Rinsed

Fervour of rain
quickly absorbed
by wood and grass.

Erupting aromas,
blessed
seed of water.

Timbre of nails
clicking a mirror.

Lovers turning over,
you and me,
our bodies wet
with eternity.

Beyond

And if I didn't see the rainbow yesterday,
that everyone's talking about,
(it seems that each of its colours were
made up of seven others,
it was the rainbow of all rainbows,
a spectacle of analyses and syntheses
as after a long hunger for the Absolute!)
And if I never see
that or any other rainbow
I shan't be sorry.
I no longer feel like rubbing my eyes
on the world's beauty,
light actually scratches them,
decomposed or not.
Phenomena's attraction takes place beyond me.

No! I'm not fully immobile.
I move inside
within the centre of the core.

Questions and answers

There was a time when I asked myself:
do I deserve to swim – light in the light?
Now I no longer ask.
Nuder than my body
is my hive
with its rhobuses black and deserted.

There was a time when I asked myself:
am I entitled to so much love?
Now, I no longer ask.
The chambers of my heart are shattered.
Only the wind fools around.

That's all I'm entitled to.
That's all I deserve.

Anonymous

Since I cannot resuscitate the first kiss,
does it matter on which street it took place?
Does it matter in which clearing you made love to me
since embraces have deserted my body?
And if these words have any virtue,
does it matter where they were written
and who wrote them?

The last moment

The branches shone intensely
and the whole valley mooed
like an immense cow
with its head turned towards the sun
and that luminous moo
was the last thing I heard
before evening fell.

Then in the profound anonymity
events continued even more strangely:
All the books opened at the same page
and that very night
it was up to me to find
the connection between
centuries and mysteries.

All these were, of course, symptoms of death
but suddenly,
the books shut
with a ferocious snap.

Language

My tongue – forked like a snake's
but without deadly intentions:
just a bilingual hissing.

Ars poetica – a polemic

I am I.
I am personal.
I am subjective, intimate, private, particular,
confessional.
All that happens,
happens to me.
The landscape I describe
is myself . . .
If you're interested
in birds, trees, rivers,
try reference books.
Don't read my poems.
I'm no indexed bird,
tree or river,
just a registered Self.

Poets

Poets.
mysterious
obvious,
helmets – inside their skulls,
shields – of cellophane,
poets,
these species, these sepias
whose self defence
is splashing ink.

At Noon

At Noon

Triumph

I'm no longer twenty!
With this exclamation
my voice connects spaces
like the leap of a superb panther!
I'm no longer twenty!
I'm rising, more and more secure,
more and more beautiful,
from the foam of approximations.
My thoughts no longer hang
on thin threads like spiders legs.
I've lost the sterile clumsiness
and the panic when contemplating infinity.
I'm no longer twenty!
The miracles amplify,
every second I face
the unseen side of the world
until fireworks of meaning
illuminate my feast!

With a triumphant smile,
I confront time
as its edged diamond
sculpts my features.

Project for a possible/
impossible fairy tale

There are no forks, no spoons
in the dwarfs' house,
no lunches, no dinners.
Actually, everyone's had enough
of the morning glories, the yellow evening poppies,
the apricots turned to brandy,
– the artificial paradise
of tiny old men.

Candles and icon lamps
everywhere.
Pitch-Black
is dead
in her grown-up bed.

The double

A narrow skull, premonitory,
ramificating in two horns
– pattern of the hunters' cabins
and of meat-eating hoards.

The blue flame of alcohol,
the shadow, diaphanous dance,
flowing restlessly on the naked wall
and wet like a wound, the glass in my hands.

The circumstance flickers. Outside, maybe
a snow storm, summer, something to cull.
Maybe for centuries, I've been watching this strange place
staring at my own skull.

Serene

Serene coming back
inside parentheses;
the rings of the kind snake
which lost its green gems.

Serene coiling on the oval egg,
sleepy, submissive,
to protect it from the voracious bird
and the poking animal.

A smooth arm without a hand,
eight times around itself,
no longer menaced by colours,
just a branch of old flesh

and oblivion, oblivion . . .

Fish to fish

To communicate through the sea
ear to ear,
fish to fish,
with coins of shells on your closed eyelids
as on the dead.

To escape world's history
which gallops somewhere,
far from us blue, pallid ones.

To forget the breathing,
that to-ing and fro-ing
of our restless souls.

To forget . . .

The lamp on the bedside table

You provided me
with a soul of tea.
(Indeed, I was coming
with bony hand,
with muddy pen,
from the realm below)

Tender swamps
flicker at your foot.
Is it
a circle of temptation
or something else?

Anyway, I'm scared
by that word, climbing at a mysterious angle
like a green dew-worm
on your cylindrical ankle.

The menace

Enter the cuckoo clock,
enter its melody
as if a bird,
as if the secret of the being itself.

Don't forget to milk it regularly
when the udders, the brownish testicles
descend, heavy with time's semen.

Watch its black indicators
as if frowning eyebrows.

A proper way to vanish

I thought
I was easy to recognize
by my frail ring-finger
(now crooked),
by the feathery dog
that goes around with me.

I thought I could be
a fringe on your lamp shade,
my dear Madam Decrepitude.

No posture fits me.
The sand gnaws at my contour
until I vanish.

Grin

In midsummer,
the dry leaves
impose their crusty duration.
They scratch the table cloth,
hide sometimes behind new generations
then, suddenly, show their hag faces
grinning yellowish, brownish.
They're very stable in withering,
consistent in aggressiveness.

There's just one thing I'll say:
The tenacious leaves
have wrinkles and beaks and claws.
Like most of us,
they're getting ugly with age.
Like some of us
they're immortal.

Vegetal nightmare

Viola, terrifying flower with eyes, with mouth, and with moustache,
you're multiplied in crazy portraits by some pale gardener, quite dull;
he made a tribe, crepuscular, in scary colours; purple eyebrows
above the empty eye sockets. Is it a flower? Or a skull?

Just like that

Like that, just like that, twisting myself, crouching,
grimacing like a blade of grass on fire,
that's my lot when climbing
the so called steps of perfection,
while others pass like angels, waltzing,
on one shoulder a wedding cake
and on the other a barbell,
moon at one end, sun at the other.

Burning flowers

Thin stamens like lightbulb filaments,
some blue flames, some red,

– but I'm not allowed to burn in flowers
because, see, malevolence occurs.

Wherever I try to hide myself,
malevolence follows me like a trail
soiling my peace of mind,
threatens the place where I plant my pencil,
down to the roots of candid astonishment,
down to the roots of these flowers
exempt of ashes.

If, inadvertently, I did provoke an eruption
of derision and hatred
just by passing by with burning flowers
in my hand
– it's too late now to change my trade,
for instance to sell record players
or butterfly antennae smelling of alcohol.

Flowers burn in my hand
despite the raining globs of spit.

Boiling

I promised myself
never again to enter the melting pot
But what can I do?
I'm already inside.
On my cheeks – onion saliva,
celery's pittle.
I am the stew.

That event

The eighty year-olds
the victors,
look at us and smile.
They watch our vivacious legs,
our ambitious eyes,
listen to our gleaming voices
– and smile.

They move slowly,
their destination is within,
they try not to shake
the water in the glass,
the soul in the body,
the look in the eyes.

They glide into sleep
and from sleep into waking
with very little surprise
because nothing that happens to them
is for the first time
– as for the unknown event,
the one they've never experienced,
that event . . .

Mythology

Lemur,
spirit of the dead,
breezes over me,
dries up the sea's slobber
on my body,
cools off my blood,
cures me of the five senses.

Loving you, longing for you,
– that's all I am.
Sagittarius – he vanished:
only his platinum arrow
points at your abstraction.

Pressure

If a tear is
the egg of the rain-bird,
if the bird is
air's anxiety
if the air itself is
a body covering bodies
how am I ever supposed to write a book
in this common grave?

Dedication

And if the flesh is disappointed
(in fact crushed, smashed and hacked)
the spirit stays, that green alcohol
of the fruit I once impersonated.

Read my book and get dizzy
on the fragrance of my flesh.

At Night

Performances

He overtook a cruiser in a tiny boat.
He burst through a window without breaking it.
He jumped in the street with one sock tied to the other.
He claimed to have eight dads yet no mother.

He unscrewed mountains. He licked pollen,
He boasted the exact number of nerves in a cat.
Always elated, never sullen,
he knew he deserves all he gets.

He was even capable of packing a carpet in a
                                    very small tube.

So, she fell in love with him – heard wedding bells!

But then his ego began to sneeze.
And apart from sneezing
he couldn't do much else.

The frog and me

I chat to the frog.
I treat him courteously
so as not to hear his croak
because I can't stand rudeness or vulgarity.
The frog smiles amorously, touches me
with his damp paws,
and shares a terrible secret
which could kill me instantly.

I listen to it
right to the end of it.
I don't know how to protect myself.
The only thing to do is fake attention and gratitude.
And then the frog, thinking himself the master,
spares me,
by losing interest.

Thrillers

The cylindrical, the spherical witness,
and it's enough for everything to fall into darkness,
for the jurors to forget their lucid opinions
and nobody knows any more
who killed who
who will kill who
and the verdict is postponed *sine die*
in eternal confusion.

Only the victim and the murderer in fact
know who's who, from first to last act.

Conspiracies

The cetacean, apparently calm,
has an eye of napalm,
dives at predictable intervals,
with a sort of continuity
that makes you fall asleep,
destroys your vigilance
and paddles you in its direction.

The agencies have three letters
(or two or four),
they control the mammal
like a robot with eggplant coloured skin,
make its nostrils eject
superb, fairy like artesian wells
and want you to believe
Kennedy died of natural causes.

At the fun fair

Where does it come from,
this blackening under my nails?
I, the neat one, the clean one,
since when has dirt been endeared to me?

The most elaborate dignity
is invaded by the sordid swarm
(bred in a fly's intestine),
the enemy installs his sign
and it's a feast, an incredible party,
every sound conducted
by an orchestra of machine guns.

A burning curtain,
purple and pierced with sequins,
depicts the fair's Holy Mother.

Nothing matches – sacred, profane,
the merry-go-round, the hangman, the insect.
But don't worry.
in the end, the syllogism turns out to be perfect.

Stuck

Once, we emerged howling
from the sea, filled with medusas;
screaming, we extirpated ourselves
from that lumpy, insidious glue
under the moon – itself a jellyfish squashed on the sky –
and in vain our bodies were
naked, luscious, wanton.
Nausea smeared our love.

Then, remember? The storm was whipping and slapping us
and I said, maybe this is purification
(we needed it so badly)
maybe we are rinsing ourselves of ourselves –
but no,
we were not to be redeemed.
Our sins were hanging
from the corners of our eyes
like nettles.

Equality

If I dress up like a peacock,
you dress like a kangaroo.
If I make myself into a triangle,
you acquire the shape of an egg.
If I were to climb on water,
you'd climb on mirrors.

All our gestures
belong to the solar system.

Of no consequence

Good-bye – no sequel to the fairy tale,
tin man with rigid joints, covered with dust.
Why aren't I kissing your metal mouth?
Because it could rust.

I abandoned you somewhere
at the crossroad of Wrongway and Noguide
– like a medieval armour
with a rotten hero inside.

Escape from reign

Huge agitated creatures
haunt my window.
I try not to look
but my sight is yanked out
by disorded limbs.
I tell myself: It's the wind,
just the wind with arms and legs.
But I notice the tree's convulsion,
the epileptic leaves
struggling in the storm.

Vegetal nature abandons its reign,
Shudders like a green dog in its sleep,
shakes like a big ape.
The landscape fills with howling.

Sex bombshell

They were only eighteen, their thighs
like stuffed bustards, their breasts –
fanatic like military helmets.
their black braids – running pitch,
their red hair – orchestra stalls,
their blonde strand – saxophones.

They were only eighteen, but in their eyes
you could see battles, thistles,
and engines for chopping violins.
Oh, those eyes! With such strict perimeters
that the once sensitive nomenon
blinked full of fear – an animal core
hairy with eyelashes as if phenomena.
They were only eighteen
but smashed between pages, they seemed
already old and ready
for the great funeral parade of beauty.
You could imagine their bones inside their flesh
dying on the page's white stretcher
arousingly – at the age of eighteen.

The fourth monkey

In the well-known 'sitting' position
like the Three Monkeys – the One Who Doesn't See,
the One Who Doesn't Hear, the One Who Doesn't Speak –
with my cigarette's ash falling on my naked thighs,
with the sea before me
and death behind,
I test between my teeth a syllable of eternity,
as if a suspect coin.

My nails are narrowing.
My fingers thickening.
They don't flow anymore
under the broken bridge of my rings.

I am the Monkey Who is Sentenced to Write.

Piano in frost

On the keyboard, my freezing hands,
captive waterlilies,
frail stems stockstill in the lake.
It's my first assassinated fragment.
Soon, you'll contemplate
my frostbitten knees,
the glazed crust on my eyes
like a definitive contact lens
and you'll hear my cells cracking
– before the appearance of my perfected skeleton:
a solemn, silver church organ.

Three dialogues

Stanza

The letters in my name were hoping for
a winning, with their lucky number: 'four'.

– Will you be back, my lover? – Nevermore
croaks Poe himself, buried in Baltimore.

II

No future

– So I'll die without contemplating the Rocky Mountains . . .
– Probably, says Iguana, you can't have it all.
You saw the big orange peeling itself at dawn,
you saw the morbid waters of Venice
slowly devouring beauty,
you saw letters crawling and ruining concepts,
you saw the emerald in my goitre.
– That means I won't see the Rocky Mountains . . .
– Probably not, says Iguana
. . . until further notice.

III

Sonorities

– Is 'Sophomore' a soporific?
– No.
– Is 'glibly' a squirrel
and 'serendipity' a caterpillar?
– No, of course not.
– Is 'perfunctory' the dining room
of an abbey?
– No, not at all.

– Then, why do you mislead me?
Just because I'm a foreigner?

Interdiction

Just what are you doing here in transparent clothes
raising a cupful of words
to the indifferent lips of time?
Who was it lied to you
that morasses long for the moon
and that a bird dances
in the centre of the earth?
Why don't you just accept rejection,
why don't you just tie your legs,
tight, tight, one against the other?
For what's going on around you
is no longer your concern.

Thoughts on a stretcher

I'm truly sorry that I won't attend
the solemn hour – with a limpid mind.
Thick fog surrounds my present, drowns me
in an (exempt of grandeur), nothingness.
I wished I had pronounced the Syllable,
I wished for the Primordial Sound, so that
the fish's ear, the deafened one, could hear me,
the White Owl to be startled in her sleep.
I wished I'd drawn a Testament of air
and closed my eyes in sweet consent,
on an enamoured, final look.

But no. I cannot speak, I cannot see.
the world
distantly
turns its back on me.

Cheerleader for a funeral

Everything was amazement
in that wretched adolescence:
the cheap hotel room,
the sleet, the buses
crowded with indifferent people.
Everything had a taste and a smell:
the coffee cake, my green damp coat,
not to mention the ridiculous beret
on my oblong skull
– like a miniscule hat
on a circus dog.

Never mind, let's do it all again,
let's get amazed, let's celebrate
the trash, the unusable matches,
the streets suffocated by confused hatred
– though the girl is now a hag –
let's be amazed, let's yell
at the great festivities of multiple decrepitude:
one falls,
        one winters.

I cannot die

Under the blue snowfalls I
tried so many times to die
listening to my sad blood
slowly freezing deep inside
and if – look – I didn't die
possibly it was because
snow had stopped halfway – who knows?
or, perhaps that love, alack,
with a vengeful smile came back
and defrosted me and got,
crawling, right into my blood,
in my meninx, deep inside.

Snow again. Blue as before.
I no longer try to die.
No, not anymore.

Poems in
Original
Manuscript

A comunica prin mare
ureche lîngă ureche,
~~șold lîngă șold~~ pește lîngă pește.
în ~~tacid~~ ~~de complet~~
cu ochii deschiși,
(scria pește)
ca la morți,
~~scufundați~~
a ~~fugi~~ ~~de~~ lumina de afară,
(de istoria lumii,
~~și țopăi~~ ~~pe~~
~~care~~ ~~de tropotul ei tot mai depărtat~~
care tropăie undeva, [departe
→ ~~de mine și de tine,~~
de noi, cei verzi și vineți
A uita de respirație.
de acel du-te vino
al sufletului nostru neliniștit
și a uita... și trecător,

━

Fish to fish (page 27)

Am crezut
că sînt ușor de recunoscut
după gingașul meu inelar
(acum încîrjat)
și după cîinele cu pene
care mă moațește.
Am crezut că pot fi
un ciucure la abajurul Dumneavoastră;
Doamnă De crepitu dine.
Nu-mi reușește nici o postură.
Îți pierd nai routăaie conturul.
Dispar,
mă fac una cu el.

A proper way to vanish (page 30)

Cîndva mă-ntrebam dacă mi se cuvine
să-not în lumină și limpezime
-acum nu mă-ntreb.

~~Dar nici bucurie nu este~~

Mai gol decît trupul
mi-e ~~cuvântul gândul~~
stupul.
cu toate rombunile pustii.
Cîndva mă-ntrebam negre și: demnă sont oare
de-atîta iubire?
Acum nu mă-ntreb
Sînt sparte-ncăperile inimii.
Suflă vîntul printre ele.
De-atîta sînt demnă
și-atîta mi se cuvine.

≥

Questions and answers (page 15)